PUZZLES

by Dava Walker

Illustrated by
Cornelius Van Wright
and Ying-Hwa Hu

Foreword by
William H. Schultz, M.H.S., P.A.-C.
and Ruth A. Smullin

Lollipop Power Books   Carolina Wren Press   Durham, North Carolina

Project Director and Editor: Ruth A. Smullin

Medical Consultant: William H. Schultz, M.H.S., P.A.-C.

Art Director: Martha Scotford

Consulting Editor: Jacqueline K. Ogburn

Walker, Dava Jo, 1955-
Puzzles/Dava Jo Walker; illustrated by Cornelius Van Wright
and Ying-Hwa Hu; foreword by William H. Schultz and Ruth A. Smullin.
p. cm.
Summary: Nine-year-old Cassie tries to complete a school
project while coping with the pain and fatigue of sickle cell anemia.
ISBN 0-914996-29-0 (pbk.)
1. Sickle cell anemia -- Juvenile literature. [1. Sickle cell anemia.]
I. Van Wright, Cornelius, ill. II. Hu, Ying-Hwa, ill. III. Title.
RC641.7.S5W35   1996
362.1'98921527 -- dc20   95-39033   CIP   AC

For Kit - DW

      To Maria D. Lites - CVW & YH

For my daughters - RAS

      To the children and families coping with sickle
cell disease - WHS

Michelle,
May your life be filled
with butterflies.
Love,
Dava

Special thanks to our funders

The publication of *Puzzles* was made possible
by a generous grant
from Ronald McDonald Children's Charities,
"lifting kids to a better tomorrow."

Additional funding was provided
by the Duke Children's Miracle Network.

Carolina Wren Press and Lollipop Power Books
gratefully acknowledge the ongoing support
made possible in part through gifts
to the Durham Arts Council's
United Arts Fund.

Acknowledgments

We are grateful to the many individuals and organizations whose contributions of time and thought were essential to this project.

We thank Shelley Day, former Executive Director, Carolina Wren Press, for her work on a first draft of the grant proposal; and John Falletta, M.D., Professor of Pediatrics, Hematology-Oncology, Duke University Medical Center, for his helpful suggestions regarding a later version of the proposal.

Many people reviewed the story manuscript and gave us the benefit of their insights. For this we thank M. Anita Holmes, M.P.H., J.D., former Education Director, Duke-UNC Comprehensive Sickle Cell Center; Bettye Kelly, M.S.W., parent of a sickle cell child and a member of the Community Advisory Board, Duke-UNC Comprehensive Sickle Cell Center; Vivian Lewis, M.S., Certified Child Life Specialist, Duke University Medical Center; Victoria Odesina, R.N., M.S., University of Connecticut St. Francis Sickle Cell Service, and parent of a sickle cell child; Cheryl Reddish, M.L.S., Assistant Professor, North Carolina Central University School of Library and Information Science; and Felicia Tate of Durham, N.C., sickle cell patient and parent of a sickle cell child.

We thank the following for the enthusiastic endorsements they wrote in support of our grant proposal: Kwaku Ohene Frempong, M.D., President of the Sickle Cell Disease Association of America, Inc.; the International Association of Sickle Cell Nurses and Physician Assistants; Thomas R. Kinney, M.D., Co-Director Duke-UNC Comprehensive Sickle Cell Center; Kermit Nash, Ph.D., Professor of Social Work, University of North Carolina at Chapel Hill; and Clarice Reid, M.D., Director, Division of Blood Diseases and Resources of the National Heart, Lung and Blood Institute of the National Institutes of Health.

For detailed information on particular species of butterflies and on plants used in butterfly gardens, we are grateful to Patricia Collins, Director of Education, and Lu Ann Craighton, Interpretive Naturalist, both at the Cecil B. Day Butterfly Center, Callaway Gardens, Pine Mountain, Georgia.

And last but not least, we are grateful to Alex Gordon, former Director of Child Life Programs at Duke University Medical Center, who suggested to Ruth Smullin that Bill Schultz might be interested in her idea, thus setting the whole thing in motion.

Every one of you helped make this book a reality.

Ruth A. Smullin
William H. Schultz

The illustrators gratefully acknowledge the following individuals for all their help: Lennette Benjamin, M.D.; Jean Lagomarsino, R.N., M.A.; Gwendolyn Pittman, R.N.; Eva Radel, M.D.; Fred Stern, M.D.; and Gwendolyn Swinson, R.N.; as well as the staff of the Montefiore Medical Center.

Cornelius Van Wright
Ying-Hwa Hu

To the adult reading this book with a child

Puzzles is a story about Cassie, a school-age child with sickle cell disease. Her physical difficulties are common to children with this inherited blood disorder. Her illness also affects her feelings about herself, her friends, her family and others. A supportive adult, reading *Puzzles* to a child, can provide an opportunity to talk about feelings that surface in the course of the reading. The adult can reassure the child that the feelings are normal and, when possible, can suggest positive ways to respond to trying situations. Cassie's problems are not trivial, but the support and help of her parents allow her to achieve some mastery over particular difficulties as they arise.

Whether the child reading *Puzzles* has sickle cell disease, is unaffected, or has some other chronic illness, the story can help to expand the child's awareness of children like Cassie. Be prepared to listen without criticism to the child's response to the story. Be supportive by making comments that let your listener know that Cassie's feelings are real and important. Children are not fooled by adult efforts to pretend things are fine when they are not. Take the child's wishes and fears seriously. If the child is unable or unwilling to talk about feelings, you can help by naming feelings related to the story. For example, you can say, "It's really hard when you have to miss school so much. I know you hate being away from your friends." Or "Does this remind you of anything that has happened to you? Or "Boy, Cassie was really angry. I don't blame her. I would have been, too."

Cassie's story shows a traditional family, with parents who are there with her through most of her health crises. Their availability and understanding promote positive thinking. In cases where parents are not available, or where circumstances make coping difficult for the parent(s), children need the support of teachers, health care providers and members of the extended family. Teachers can be especially helpful, since they may be the first to be aware of emotional, social and academic problems arising from frequent school absences. In *Puzzles*, the author has included the most typical physical and emotional problems of sickle cell disease. Cassie's situation may be different from the reader's. Not all families have the same resources. Many children with sickle cell disease have more serious physical and emotional problems, and some have fewer. Nonetheless, both the story and the discussion below can suggest helpful ways of communicating.

Fatigue and Pain. Cassie's complaints of being tired and having aches and pains are the most common complaints of children with sickle cell disease. Although often vague, these are real physical symptoms. Playmates and adults may discount them because they are also common among healthy children who are bored or disinterested. It is normal for the sickle cell child to feel anger and frustration at being different and unable to keep up physically with friends and classmates.

Small Stature. The growth of children with sickle cell disease may be delayed, making them smaller than others the same age and frequent targets of unkind remarks. Teasing and frequent absences from school can cause loss of self-esteem and exclusion from group activities by other children. Cassie deals with Martin by ignoring him, which is often the best way to discourage teasing. However, she does not ignore her own feelings. She recognizes that she is angry. But instead of dwelling on her anger, she focuses her attention on her science project, which makes her feel good.

Myths. Children hear many warnings about contagious diseases in television advertising, in the movies and at school. It is natural for Martin to think Cassie's disease is contagious. This misunderstanding can cause children to avoid the child with sickle cell disease, thus increasing her isolation. Cassie is appropriately angry when Martin teases her, and she speaks out in a helpful way. She tells Martin she is angry and also corrects his misunderstanding. It was helpful for Cassie to know some basic facts about her illness and also to feel comfortable telling her friend that he hurt her feelings.

Disruption of Routine. The chronic and unpredictable nature of sickle cell disease often interferes with planned activities. Cassie's trip is ruined because of fever. Fever is a sign of infection, a leading cause of death in sickle cell children. It may be hard for the child with sickle cell disease to understand the seriousness of fever, especially because parental reaction to fever in an unaffected sibling is very different. Cassie is angry and sad because she cannot go to Atlanta. Her mother is firm about the need to go to the clinic, but she acknowledges Cassie's anger and the unfairness of the situation.

Trait Vs. Disease. Sickle cell trait occurs in one out of every ten African-Americans. Sickle cell trait is not the disease. It can never "turn into" the disease.

The Sickled Cell. Cassie is not too young to learn about the cause of her symptoms. With the microscope, she can see the "banana-shaped" cells and compare them to normal blood cells. The misshapen cells are not as flexible as normal cells and tend to clog small blood vessels. The clogging is the cause of pain associated with sickle cell disease. Dr. Lewis recognizes that information about her illness can help Cassie deal with her frustration.

Coping. The excruciating pain events of sickle cell disease can be terrifying to a child. The child has little control over these events and may feel hopeless or depressed. The worse the pain, the more negative the feelings. In the face of the severity of this problem, it is a challenge for a family to promote positive thinking, and it is not always possible. Cassie's parents encourage her to succeed by being flexible and finding ways to make alternative plans when necessary. By focusing on what Cassie "can do," they suggest an alternative to her feelings of defeat and show a more hopeful way of coping.

In *Puzzles*, Cassie's parents and doctor show ways to listen to, nurture and encourage children with chronic disease to do the best that they can.

Ziggedy-zaggedy black cracks had turned our school playground into a giant jigsaw puzzle. I scuffed my shoe against the cracks and wondered if the asphalt puzzle would come apart smoothly.

"Pull up that piece," I told my little brother. "The one that looks like Texas."

"No way," said Samuel.

"It's like a puzzle. It will go right back together."

"Then you do it," he said.

"I'm tired and my back hurts. You pull."

"You're always tired," Samuel complained.

Other first graders were curling their fingers around the hot, tarry-smelling asphalt. They pulled out Texas and then started working on another piece.

"Hey, Cassie," Sarah called from where my fourth-grade classmates were playing kickball. "Why are you hanging around the little kids?"

"She's with the shrimpboats 'cause she is one," Martin jeered.

My cheeks felt hot. I pretended to ignore him, but he was right. I am nine years old, but I'm only a little bigger than the first graders.

The little kids were still trying to put the playground puzzle back together when I saw the principal coming.

"Cassandra, this is your last warning," Mrs. Danielson said. "Stop putting the first graders up to pranks. Go join your own class."

I looked at Mrs. Danielson. Even in her flat shoes she was the tallest person at school. What did she know about having sickle cell disease and being called "shrimpboat"?

By the time I reached my classroom, I had forgotten about being mad at Martin and Mrs. Danielson. I had almost forgotten how much my back hurt. This was the day we were choosing from Mr. Carrera's list of science projects. I rushed to sign up for "animal behavior."

"What animal are you going to study, Cassie?" Sarah asked.

"Butterflies. My dad says he'll take me to the butterfly center near Atlanta. It has a giant garden full of flowers that butterflies like. When you stand still, they land right on you."

I closed my eyes and imagined myself in the butterfly garden. If I stood as still as a statue under a sassafras tree, would spicebush swallowtails land on my sleeves? Would a dozen painted ladies flutter against my hair like ribbons in the wind?

"She should study shrimp," said Martin.

I opened my eyes. Why was Martin always making fun of me? I wished I was big enough to give him a good hard shove.

"You want a partner?" Sarah asked.

"Watch out," said Martin. "You might catch her sick cells."

"I don't have sick cells. I have sickle cell disease, and it's not contagious."

Mr. Carrera clapped his hands. "Listen up, gang. You have two weeks to complete your projects. Think of it as solving a puzzle. Read books about your subject, and you'll find the pieces you need to put your puzzle together."

The only piece missing from my puzzle was a visit to the butterfly garden.

But the next day, I was on my way to the sickle cell clinic, not the butterfly garden.

"It's not fair," I said. "I hate these old sickle cells."

"You're right, honey," said Mama. "It isn't fair. But let's see what happens at the clinic. Maybe your fever will go down, and Dr. Lewis won't have to keep you long at the hospital."

She smoothed the hair from my forehead and handed me a warm, wrinkled handkerchief.

"Mama, this is the only weekend Daddy is driving to Atlanta." I wiped away the tears that hadn't already found my shirt. "We were going to see the butterflies."

"I know, Cassie. But your health is more important. You'll think of a new science project. Samuel and I will help you."

"Samuel's too young to help," I said.

After Mama checked me in at the clinic, a nurse took us to a room for some tests. Even though I've had this stuff a million times, I still hate the needles. I closed my eyes while the nurse took my blood. I thought about my brother and how skinny he was.

"Mama, are you sure Samuel won't get sickle cell disease?"

"I'm sure," she answered, squeezing my hand. "Samuel did inherit sickle cell trait, but that is not the same as the disease. It can never become sickle cell disease."

"Well," I said, closing my eyes again as the nurse brought the IV needles, "that's one good thing, anyway."

There was nothing good about the next day. Daddy was in Atlanta alone, and I was in the hospital.

Mama had just gone to get a cup of tea when someone knocked on my door.

"Come in," I called. The door opened a crack, and Dr. Lewis peeked in.

"Good morning," she said. "Your mom told me you missed a trip to Atlanta to observe butterflies, so I brought you something else to look at."

"What is it?"

Dr. Lewis smiled. "It's something so small you need a microscope to see it."

She opened the door wider and pulled a cart into my room. A microscope sat on top. Dr. Lewis helped me adjust the eyepiece, and I peered through the microscope lens.

"What are those red blobs?" I asked.

"Blood cells," said Dr. Lewis. "The ones shaped like bananas are the sickle cells."

"You mean I'm sick because my blood went bananas?"

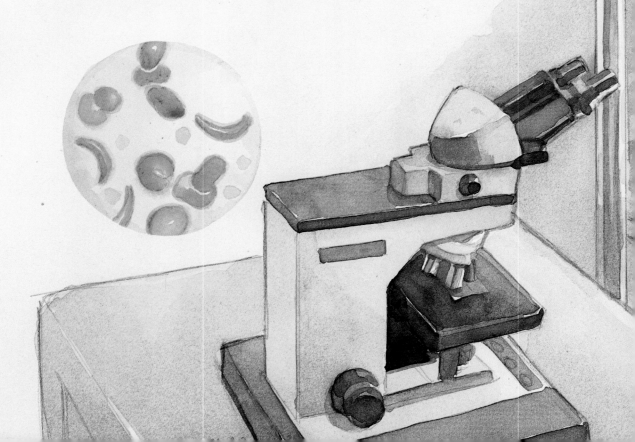

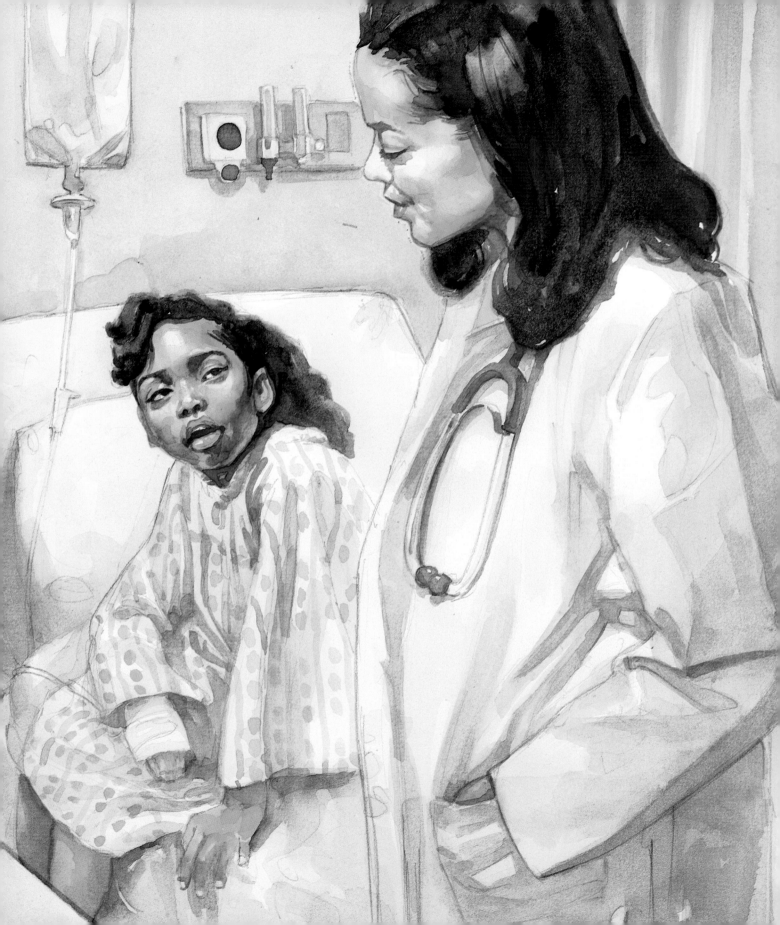

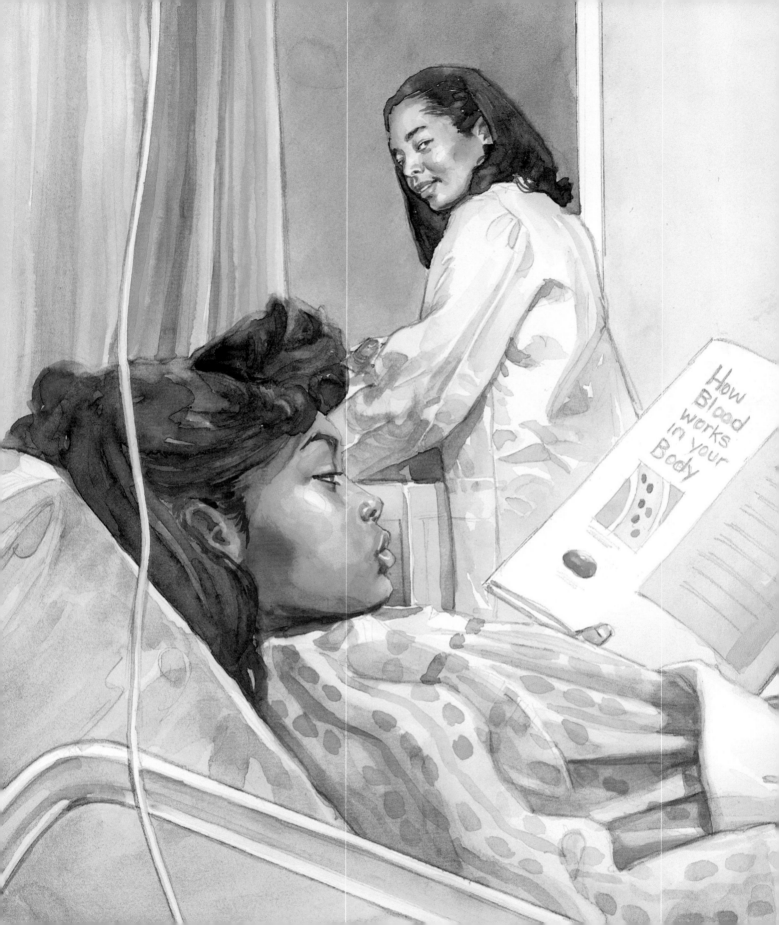

Dr. Lewis laughed. "That's one way of putting it. And the puzzle for doctors – what drives us bananas – is trying to figure out how to stop those cells from making you sick."

"But this won't help me with my animal behavior project."

"Well," Dr. Lewis said, "all animals are made up of cells, and every animal, even a delicate butterfly, has to have blood cells in order to live. Maybe you could study blood cells."

I shrugged.

She handed me a book. "Even if you don't want to do your project on blood cells, you might like reading about how blood works in your body. I'll see you tomorrow."

The next day, Daddy came to the hospital with booklets about the butterfly center and a video he had made.

"I rented a camcorder," he said as he adjusted the VCR in the patient lounge. "It's almost as good as being there."

"Thanks, Daddy," I said.

We pushed and pulled my IV pole to a big chair so I could watch the video from Daddy's lap. The butterflies on the tape were so beautiful they made me cry. Daddy hugged me tight and I cried harder.

"I wanted to go with you. I wanted to see them myself."

"I know, honey." He handed me a tissue.

I blew my nose. "I'm tired of being sick and hurting all the time. I'm tired of missing school and being stuck in this stupid old hospital."

"I'm sorry you miss out on so much," said Daddy. "I missed having you with me yesterday, but I'll be staying here with you tonight. And Dr. Lewis said if your fever is down, you can come home tomorrow."

The next day I was back in my own bed trying to write about blood cells.

"My hand hurts too much, Mama," I said. "I can't even write. I'll just have to flunk science."

"Oh, no, you don't," said Mama. "I know your hand hurts, and I know you feel bad about missing the butterfly garden. But I also know I'm not raising any quitters."

"How can I finish my project when I can't write?"

"You're a smart girl, Cassie. Don't tell me what you can't do. Tell me what you can do."

I pulled my coverlet over my head and pretended I was a chrysalis in my cocoon. Soon, I thought, I will be a beautiful monarch butterfly, instead of an ugly old sickle cell.

I stared up at my coverlet. The patchwork colors were lit by the sun like a stained-glass window. One square of fabric had bright yellow trumpets. They reminded me of the honeysuckle flowers that some butterflies love, which reminded me of Daddy's video. And that gave me an idea.

A week later I was walking to the front of my class to give my science report. I felt nervous and queasy. I slid my video into the VCR and sat down to watch with the rest of the class. There I was on television, acting just like a TV news reporter.

"This is Cassandra Gooding with today's special segment on sickle cell disease," I was saying. "You already know some things about sickle cell disease because you know some things about me. I'm small for my age and I'm tired a lot. I can't

always keep up with my friends on the playground, and sometimes I miss school because I have fevers and pain and have to go to the hospital. This report will tell you more about sickle cell disease."

My classmates watched me interview the experts: Dr. Lewis, other kids with sickle cell disease, Mama and Daddy, even Samuel. When my video was finished, some kids were staring at me, but not the way they usually stare. Some of them looked puzzled and some looked surprised. Martin even looked a little bit sorry.

"Hey, Cassie," Sarah called when we reached the playground at recess, "do you really get to watch TV all day when you're in the hospital?"

"Yeah," I said, "but I still hate being there."

"Why?"

"For one thing, they're always poking me with needles, giving me shots and taking blood. And I miss playing with my friends."

"I'll visit you if you have to go again," Sarah said. "Isn't it scary being all alone in the hospital at night?"

"Oh, I'm never alone at night. There are doctors and nurses around, and my mom or dad always sleeps right beside me in the room."

Suddenly, a stampede of fourth graders rounded the
school building and almost knocked us down. They were
shouting and running toward the edge of the playground.

"Come on, shrimpboat," Martin yelled. "They're filling the
cracks with tar today."

I grabbed Sarah's hand, and we ran to catch up with the
others.

Resources

THINGS TO READ

*National Sickle Cell Mutual Help
Directory*
The Psychosocial Research Program of
the Duke University/University of
North Carolina Comprehensive Sickle
Cell Center
School of Social Work
301 Pittsboro Street, CB # 3550
Chapel Hill, NC 27599-3550
919-966-5932 phone
919-962-0890 fax

*A Parent's Handbook for Sickle Cell
Disease: Part I - Birth to Six Years of Age*
*A Parent's Handbook for Sickle Cell
Disease: Part II - Six to Eighteen Years of
Age*
National Maternal and Child Health
Clearinghouse
2070 Chain Bridge Road, Suite 450
Vienna, VA 22182-2536
703-821-8955, ext. 254 or 265 phone
703-821-2098 fax

*Sickle Cell Disease Related Pain,
A Guide for Patients and Parents:
Assessment and Management*
New England Regional Genetics Group
P.O. Box 670
Mt. Desert, ME 04660
207-288-2704 phone
207-288-2705 fax

*Sickle Cell Disease: The Teacher Can
Make a Difference*
Duke University Comprehensive Sickle
Cell Center
Duke University Medical Center
Box 2916
Durham, NC 27710
919-684-3401 phone
919-681-7950 fax

PLACES TO CALL FOR HELP

Boston City Hospital
Comprehensive Sickle Cell Center
818 Harrison Avenue, FGH-2
Boston, MA 02118
617-534-5727 phone
617-534-5739 fax

The Children's Hospital of Philadelphia
Comprehensive Sickle Cell Center
34th Street and Civic Center Boulevard
Philadelphia, PA 19104
215-590-3423 phone
215-590-2499 fax

College of Physicians and Surgeons
Columbia University
Comprehensive Sickle Cell Center
630 West 168th Street
New York, NY 10032
212-305-6531 phone
212-305-8408 fax

Duke University Comprehensive Sickle
Cell Center
Duke University Medical Center
Box 2916
Durham, NC 27710
919-684-3401 phone
919-681-7950 fax

Emory University School of Medicine
Comprehensive Sickle Cell Center
Department of Medicine
69 Butler Street, NE
Atlanta, GA 30335
404-616-3572 phone
404-616-5998 fax

International Association of Sickle Cell
Nurses and Physician Assistants
P.O. Box 63005
800 Madison Avenue
Memphis, TN 38163

Meharry Medical College
Department of Pediatrics
Comprehensive Sickle Cell Center
1005 Dr. D.B. Todd Jr. Boulevard
Nashville, TN 37208
615-327-6763 phone
615-327-6008 fax

Montefiore Medical Center
Comprehensive Sickle Cell Center
111 East 210th Street
Bronx, NY 10467
718-920-7373 phone
718-798-5095 fax

Sickle Cell Disease Association of
America
200 Corporate Pointe, Suite 495
Culver City, CA 90230-7633
310-216-6363 phone
310-215-3722 fax

Sickle Cell Disease Research
Foundation
4401 South Crenshaw Boulevard
Suite 208
Los Angeles, CA 90043
213-299-3600 phone
213-299-3605 fax

Sickle Cell Disease Scientific Research
Group
Division of Blood Diseases and
Resources
National Heart, Lung, and Blood
Institute
6701 Rockledge Drive, MSC 7950
Bethesda, MD 20892-7950
301-435-0055 phone
301-480-0868 fax

University of California
Comprehensive Sickle Cell Center
San Francisco General Hospital
1001 Potrero Avenue
Bldg. 100, Room 331
San Francisco, CA 94110
415-206-5169 phone
415-206-3071 fax

University of South Alabama
College of Medicine
Comprehensive Sickle Cell Center
CSAB 138
Mobile, AL 36688-0002
334-460-7334 phone
334-460-6604 fax

University of Southern California
Department of Medicine
Comprehensive Sickle Cell Center
2025 Zonal Avenue, RMR 304
Los Angeles, CA 90033
213-342-1259 phone
213-342-1255 fax

ON THE INTERNET

Web sites with information about other
resources can be located by searching
under "sickle cell disease."

Dava Walker learned to read in Spokane, Washington, learned to write at Georgetown University, and began her career as a children's author and editor in Washington, D.C. She now lives in Princeton, New Jersey, with her husband, Kit, and their daughter, Rachel. This is her first picture book.

Cornelius Van Wright and Ying-Hwa Hu have been illustrating books together since 1989. Their 1991 book, *Make a Joyful Sound*, received a *Parenting Magazine* Reading Magic Award and the *Hungry Mind Review* Book of Distinction Award. Their 1994 book, *Zora Hurston and the Chinaberry Tree*, won the American Booksellers Association Pick of the List Award. It was selected for the 1994 Society of Illustrators Show and appeared on Public TV's *Reading Rainbow*. Their 1995 book, *Sam and the Lucky Money*, also won the ABA Pick of the List Award. They live in New York City with their two children.